Explore!

ANCIENT CHINA

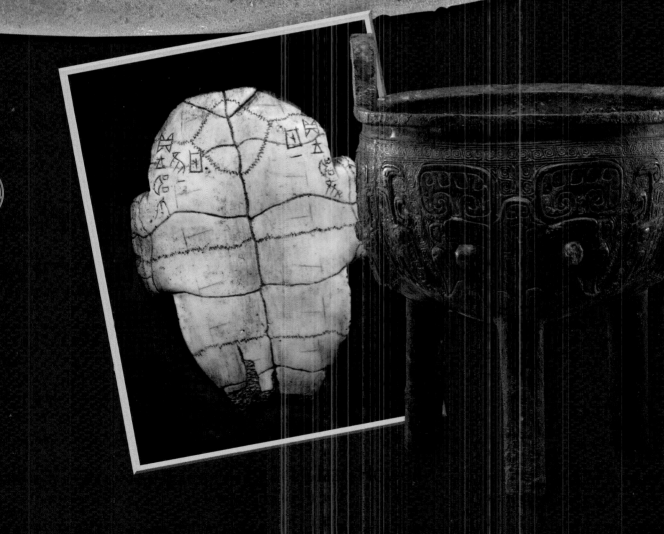

Published in Great Britain in 2018 by Wayland

ISBN 978 1 5263 0058 4

10 9 8 7 6 5 4 3 2 1

MIX
Paper from
responsible sources
FSC
www.fsc.org
FSC® C104740

Wayland
An imprint of Hachette Children's Group
Part of Hodder & Stoughton
Carmelite House
50 Victoria Embankment
London EC4Y 0DZ

An Hachette UK Company
www.hachette.co.uk
www.hachettechildrens.co.uk

A catalogue record for this title is available from the
British Library

Printed and bound in Malaysia

Produced for Wayland by
White-Thomson Publishing Ltd
www.wtpub.co.uk

Editor: Izzi Howell
Designer: Clare Nicholas
Picture researcher: Izzi Howell
Illustrations: Techtype
Wayland editor: Vicky Brooker
Consultant: Philip Parker

Picture acknowledgements:
The author and publisher would like to thank the
following agencies and people for allowing these
pictures to be reproduced:

Alamy/Granger, NYC. 6, 7 (top) and 20; Alamy/China
Images 11 (bottom); Alamy/The Art Archive 13 (top);
Alamy/TAO Images Limitedn 13 (bottom); Alamy/World
History Archive 21 (bottom); Alix Wood 19 (bottom);
Dreamstime/Jun Mu 9 (bottom) and 29 (bottom); iStock/
yipengge cover (top left) and 24; iStock/Robert_Ford
11 (top); iStock/PrinPrince 15 (top); Stefan Chabluk
7 (top); Shutterstock/zens cover (top right) and 25
(bottom); Shutterstock/Xidong Luo cover (bottom)
and 16; Shutterstock/Jun Mu title page (left) and
19 (top); Shutterstock/patpitchaya 4; Shutterstock/
sunxuejun 5 (bottom); Shutterstock/Meiqianbao 8
and 31; Shutterstock/yaipearn 9 (top); Shutterstock/
Peter Stuckings 10; Shutterstock/Mikhaylov Ilya 12;
Shutterstock/Katoosha 14; Shutterstock/joannawnuk
15 (bottom); Shutterstock/beibaoke 17 (bottom);
Shutterstock/furoking300 18; Shutterstock/Alena Brozova
21 (top); Shutterstock/Hung Chung Chih 27 (bottom) and
32; Shutterstock/Seashell World 28 (top); Shutterstock/
saknakorn 28 (bottom); Shutterstock/fotoslaz 29 (top);
Werner Forman Archive/Sold at Christies cover (centre
right); Werner Forman Archive/ Private Collection London
5 (top); Wikimedia/Xuan Che 25 (top); Wikimedia/Photo
Dharma 26; Yale University Art Gallery title page (right), 3,
17 (top), 22, 27 (top).

Design elements by Shutterstock/lalan, Shutterstock/
daniana and Shutterstock/OlichO.

Contents

Who lived in ancient China?

In ancient China, a series of dynasties (ruling families) ruled over an area in the north east of the country. The Shang dynasty controlled this area for over 500 years, from about 1600 to 1046 BCE.

The Shang kings consulted the gods to see if farmers would have a good harvest.

Under control

Shang kings were well organised. They controlled the peasants that lived in their territory and forced them to work together on large projects. These projects included building cities, digging large royal tombs and farming the land. When the Shang were under threat from other states, peasants were called up to fight in the king's army.

Bronze technology

The Shang dynasty ruled during the Chinese Bronze Age. This means that they could make tools and weapons from bronze but they did not know how to work metals such as iron. The Shang developed the technology to make intricately decorated bronze pots and weapons.

Skilled Shang craftspeople used pottery moulds to make elaborate designs on bronze pots, which were used in religious ceremonies.

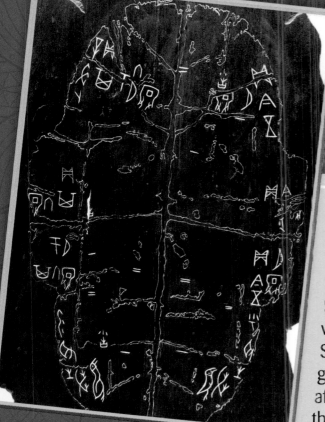

Like in modern Chinese, the Shang wrote using symbols to represent words. The symbol on this oracle bone that looks like a long 'D' means 'moon'.

How do we know

The Shang dynasty is the first Chinese dynasty that we can learn about through written evidence and artefacts. Archaeologists have found many Shang artefacts in tombs, such as bronze pots, weapons and jewellery. This is because the Shang buried members of their royal family with grave goods, objects that they would need in the afterlife. Historians have learned about life during the Shang period from the texts written on oracle bones (see page 18).

The rise of the Shang

The Shang dynasty started to rule in around 1600 BCE, after taking over from the Xia dynasty. The Shang kings were well organised and ambitious, and they kept the dynasty going for over five centuries.

This is the earliest known decorated Chinese bronze vessel. It is one of very few artefacts that dates from the time of the Xia dynasty.

The mysterious Xia

According to ancient texts written by later dynasties, the Xia was the first dynasty in the Chinese Bronze Age. They ruled an area of northern China from 2070 to 1600 BCE. However, as there are very few remains and no written records from the time of the Xia dynasty, it's hard to separate history from legend.

A new dynasty

The Xia dynasty ended in 1600 BCE when a young nobleman named Tang defeated the last Xia king, Jie. Tang made himself king of a new dynasty, known as the Shang dynasty. He built the first Shang capital city, near to the modern city of Luoyang.

This portrait of King Tang is painted on silk. It is from the early 13th century, around 2,800 years after King Tang's death.

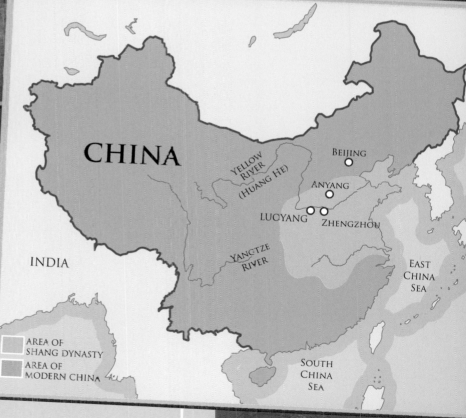

CHINA

YELLOW RIVER (HUANG HE)

BEIJING

ANYANG

LUOYANG ZHENGZHOU

INDIA

YANGTZE RIVER

EAST CHINA SEA

AREA OF SHANG DYNASTY
AREA OF MODERN CHINA

SOUTH CHINA SEA

Under Shang rule

Twenty nine different Shang kings ruled during the following 500 years. During this period, the dynasty moved its capital city around several times. The Shang people made great cultural advances, developing the beginnings of a written language and producing intricate bronze pieces.

The royal family

All of the kings in the Shang dynasty were part of the same family. Members of the royal family helped the king make important decisions.

Royal ancestors

The Shang believed that their king could communicate with his dead royal ancestors. These ancestors could then contact the supreme Shang god, Shangdi, on the king's behalf. The king had to discuss every decision about the kingdom with his royal ancestors before taking action. He also had to carry out rituals to keep his ancestors and the gods happy.

Shang kings offered their ancestors wine during rituals. This type of wine container is known as a 'gong'.

The Shang kept silkworms, a type of worm that makes threads of silk. They wove and then dyed this silk into colourful cloth, which was made into clothes for members of the royal family.

Ruling the kingdom

As well as acting as chief priest, the Shang king had to rule the kingdom. He made all the laws and organised when farmers should plant crops. He could also call up soldiers to fight in wars or order that a new capital city be built. The Shang king was supported by noblemen, many of whom were members of the royal family.

Women

When a Shang king died, his younger brother or nephew took control of the kingdom. Generally, women were not given much power. However, Lady Fu Hao, one of the wives of King Wu Ding, was an exception. She was a military leader and a priest who was allowed to carry out rituals that were normally only performed by men.

This is a modern statue of Lady Fu Hao.

Cities and buildings

Although there are no remains of Shang cities or buildings above ground, historians have learned a lot from the building foundations left beneath the ground.

City walls

Early Shang capital cities were surrounded by thick rammed-earth walls, made from layers of soil that had been pressed tightly together between two boards. The wall around the first Shang capital city was 10 metres high and 20 metres wide, and measured 7 kilometres around the city. Historians think that it would have taken 10,000 labourers working for 18 years to complete a wall of this size.

Shang earth walls were very durable. Some sections of wall still exist today in the modern Chinese city of Zhengzhou.

Changing cities

The Shang changed capital cities several times during their rule. No one knows why the Shang moved cities but it may have been due to disease or a natural disaster. Each time the Shang moved, the king forced peasants to stop farming so that they could build the new city.

Some historians think that the Shang changed their capital city because of flooding from the Yellow River.

The city of Yinxu

The biggest Shang city was Yinxu, built near the modern city of Anyang in 1200 BCE. In the city centre, wooden-framed royal palaces and temples were built on solid earth foundations. These buildings had clay walls and thatched roofs. Craftspeople lived in small houses with rammed-earth walls. Archaeologists have also found partially underground pit houses in Yinxu, which were probably the homes of peasants.

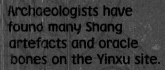

Archaeologists have found many Shang artefacts and oracle bones on the Yinxu site.

11

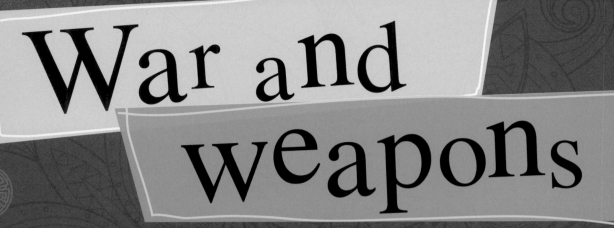

War and weapons

The Shang often fought against nomadic tribes and neighbouring states that lived in the grasslands to the west of the Shang territory. After a victory, the Shang seized valuable objects, prisoners of war for sacrifice and land for farming from their enemies.

Armies

Shang armies were made up of ordinary people, who were called away from their farms to fight as foot soldiers and noble warriors in horse-drawn chariots. Their armies often contained between 3,000 and 5,000 foot soldiers, but for a big battle, the number of foot soldiers could rise much higher. The size of their army gave the Shang a huge advantage over their enemies.

Both the Shang and nearby nomadic tribes trained horses to ride in battle.

Weapons and armour

The Shang used their knowledge of bronze technology to make bronze-tipped weapons such as battle-axes and spears. Shang bows made from wood, bone and horn could shoot arrows over a long distance. Noble warriors wore leather or bronze armour to protect their bodies and heavy bronze helmets on their heads.

This decorated bronze battle-axe was probably used by an important warrior.

Chariots

Shang kings and noblemen rode into battle in horse-drawn chariots. Each chariot had a platform with room for three people: a soldier, who drove the chariot, an archer, who fired arrows from it, and a noble warrior, who attacked with his halberd (combined spear and battle-axe). Warriors in chariots could move quickly around the battlefield, without getting stuck in hand-to-hand combat.

This is a replica of a Shang dynasty chariot.

13

Farming and food

Most ordinary Shang people worked as farmers, when they weren't away fighting in wars or building new cities. Farmers were forced to grow crops and raise animals to feed the kings and noblemen.

Crops

During the Shang era, the climate in north China was warmer and wetter than it is today. It was easy for the Shang to grow crops in the fertile land around the Yellow River. Their main crop was the grain millet, but farmers also grew wheat and rice. Other crops included vegetables such as leeks, onions and turnips.

Farmers used simple wooden or stone ox-powered ploughs to prepare the fields before planting seeds. Some farmers in China still use these farming techniques today.

Animals

Farmers raised chickens, sheep, pigs and cattle for their meat. They also hunted animals such as wild boar and muntjac deer. Fish and shellfish could be caught in the Yellow River. Kings and noblemen enjoyed hunting, but this was probably a hobby rather than a way of feeding themselves.

Muntjac deer still live in China today.

Diet

Shang kings and noblemen had a well-balanced diet, made up of grains, meat and vegetables. They were offered the finest produce from the farms and never went hungry. However, most Shang farmers didn't have a good diet, as they weren't allowed to eat all of the food that was grown. They only ate small amounts of millet and vegetables.

Shang farmers mainly ate porridge or stews made from millet.

Religion and burial

The Shang believed that the spirits of the royal ancestors lived on after death. They carried out sacrifices and rituals to please their ancestors and buried members of the royal family in elaborate tombs so that they would be happy in the afterlife.

Gods

As well as their royal ancestors, the Shang worshipped several other gods. The most important was Shangdi (Lord on high). The Shang believed that Shangdi controlled the weather and the harvest, and could cause victory or defeat in battle. Shangdi was too important to be contacted directly, even by the Shang king. The Shang king could only contact him through the spirits of the royal ancestors, who in turn, spoke to Shangdi.

The Shang also worshipped nature gods, such as the god of the Yellow River.

Sacrifices

The Shang carried out rituals and sacrifices to honour the spirits of their ancestors and to make them happy. They offered the ancestors food and wine in elaborate bronze vessels, which were specially made for these rituals. They also sacrificed animals and humans, often in cruel and brutal ways. These rituals took place regularly, according to the Shang 360-day calendar.

Wine was served from this owl-shaped bronze container during Shang rituals.

Lady Fu Hao was buried with over 2,000 items, a sign of her importance. Her tomb contained 460 bronze objects and over 750 carved jade pieces.

Burial

Members of the Shang royal family were buried in huge wooden tombs, up to 12 metres deep, as a symbol of their importance. Valuable items that the dead person would need in the afterlife were buried alongside them, including food, bronze pots, jewellery and weapons. Servants and animals were also sacrificed and buried so that they could continue to serve the dead person in the afterlife.

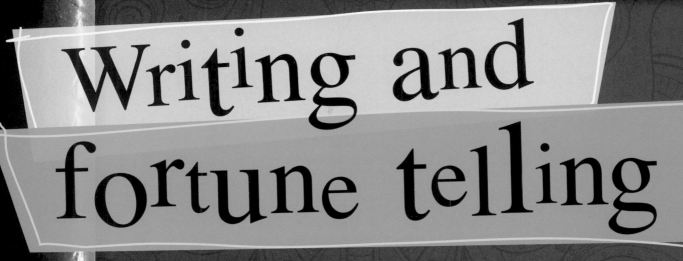

Writing and fortune telling

The Shang carved questions into animal bones as part of a fortune-telling ritual. The writing on these oracle bones has taught us a great deal about life during the Shang dynasty.

Buildings in China are often decorated with dragons, as they are a symbol of good luck and power. For this reason, dragon bones were thought to be very important.

Dragon bones

In the nineteenth century, animal bones with strange marks scratched into their surface were found in the Chinese countryside. These bones were sold to chemists as 'dragon bones' and used to make traditional Chinese medicines. One day, an ancient Chinese writing specialist noticed that the marks on the dragon bones were the same as those on ancient bronze pots. Historians realised that they were 3,000-year-old artefacts from the Shang dynasty.

Fortune telling

Oracle bones were used in rituals as a way of communicating with the royal ancestors. Questions about the future for the ancestors to answer were carved into bones. A hot piece of bronze was held against the bone to make it crack. A diviner interpreted the cracks in the bone to find out the ancestors' answer to the question.

Most oracle bones were made from turtle undershells (pictured) or the shoulder blades of oxen.

Writing

Like modern Chinese, the Shang used symbols to represent words. Some of the symbols on the oracle bones are the same as modern Chinese symbols. From the writing on the oracle bones, we have learned the names of the Shang kings and information about their cities and rituals.

The Shang symbol (left) and the modern Chinese symbol (right) for 'tree' are quite similar.

19

A day in the life

Before the Shang dynasty, people in ancient China made simple bronze objects such as knives, needles and mirrors. However, the Shang developed a new method of working with bronze that allowed them to make beautifully decorated pots and weapons. This fictional diary entry describes how a Shang craftsman would have made a bronze pot.

A Shang bronze axe-head, which would probably have been used in ritual sacrifices.

The next ceremony to please the gods is only one month away, so today is the day to start making the new bronze pot that the king ordered. The last objects I made from bronze were axes and knives, so it will be nice to make a pot for a change. Casting pots is a long and tricky process, so I'll have to work carefully.

First, I need to decide on the design of the pot. The king wants the pot to have animal shapes around the top. I'll add some spiral designs and raised dots for decoration.

Now, it's time to make the pottery moulds. The inside mould is plain, but I decorate the outside mould with all of the designs that will go on the outside of the pot. There's a lot of detail, so I spend a long time carving the mould until it's perfect.

I hear a knock at the door – a peasant has arrived with the different metal ores that are mixed together to make bronze. These ores are dug out of the ground outside of the city. I work with the other craftsmen to refine and heat the ores until we have molten bronze. I place the two moulds together and fill the gap between them with molten bronze.

Molten (liquid) bronze

I need to leave the bronze to cool down completely and set hard, so I eat a quick meal of millet, beef and vegetables while I wait. Finally, it's time to break off the moulds and see the final result. My pot has come out perfectly symmetrical – I'm so happy! I'm sure that the ancestors will be very happy when they see it full of food at the ceremony.

A Shang bronze pot

The diary entry on these pages has been written for this book. Can you create your own diary entry for another person who lived in a Shang city? It could be a member of the royal family or a peasant. Use the facts in this book and in other sources to help you write about a day in their life.

Make your own Shang bowl

The 'ding' was one of the most common shapes of Shang bronze. This was a cauldron-shaped pot with three legs and small handles. Many ding pots were decorated with a taotie (animal mask) design. You can make your own ding pot from modelling clay.

You will need:

Modelling clay

A clay modelling tool

1 Divide your modelling clay into a large ball and a small ball. Put the small ball aside. Press your thumb into the centre of the large ball until it is about 1cm from the bottom.

2 Widen the hole in the ball by pinching your fingers around the edges. Turn your bowl as you pinch so that the walls of the bowl are even.

3 Divide your small ball of clay into three large balls and four small balls. Roll the large balls into logs and attach them to the base of your bowl, using your modelling tool to smooth the join.

4

5 Add the remaining small balls of clay to the front of your bowl to make the eyes of your taotie design. Use the modelling tool to carve spirals and other designs around the rest of the bowl. Leave your bowl to air dry for 2–3 days until it is totally dry.

Handy hint
To make your ding pot look more realistic, you could paint it dark grey/green once it has dried to make it look more like bronze.

Crafts and music

In addition to elaborate bronze vessels, skilled Shang craftspeople made beautiful jade carvings and pottery. Archaeologists have also found bronze musical instruments and references to dancing and music on oracle bones.

Jade carving

The Shang valued jade for its beauty and as a symbol of wealth and power. Shang craftspeople carved jade into animal-shaped ornaments, dagger handles and elaborate weapons used in rituals. The Shang believed that jade would help dead people to live well in the afterlife, so jade ornaments were often buried in tombs.

Shang craftspeople often carved jade into the shape of animals, such as this hare.

Pottery

The Shang made hard grey pottery for everyday use. Delicate, white-glazed pots and dishes were used in their rituals, alongside bronzes. These white dishes were often decorated with the same designs as the ritual bronze pots.

This white-glazed Shang pot is decorated with a geometric pattern.

Music

We know that the Shang enjoyed music, as archaeologists have found bronze bells and drums and clay wind instruments. Bronze bells and percussion instruments were probably played during rituals and battle, to keep the soldiers moving together. Kings and noblemen enjoyed music played on clay wind instruments in their palaces.

A bronze Shang bell decorated with a taotie design.

After the Shang

Just as the Xia dynasty were overthrown by the stronger Shang dynasty, the Shang dynasty ended when the Zhou dynasty grew in power and took control.

The last Shang king

The final Shang ruler was a king named Di Xin. He came into power in 1075 BCE, and for many years, he was thought to be a wise, strong ruler. However, as time went on, Di Xin spent more time hosting parties than ruling. By the end of his rule, he was known as a bad and cruel ruler, who treated his people very unfairly.

A modern statue of Di Xin. Today, he is thought of as one of the most corrupt rulers in Chinese history.

The rise of the Zhou

As the Shang dynasty grew weaker under Di Xin, the nearby Zhou state grew stronger. They made alliances with other states and eventually attacked and defeated the Shang with an army of 45,000 men. The Zhou took over the Shang territory in 1046 BCE and ruled the Yellow River region for hundreds of years.

Like the Shang, the Zhou also used beautiful bronze vessels in rituals. Around 700 BCE, the Zhou learned how to make iron tools and weapons.

The age of the emperor

The Zhou dynasty ended after a long period of war between seven major states. In 221 BCE, the Qin dynasty took control and united the area of the seven states into one nation. Although the Qin only ruled for 15 years, they established a new government system, led by an emperor rather than a royal dynasty. Aspects of this system lasted until CE 1912, when China lost its last emperor.

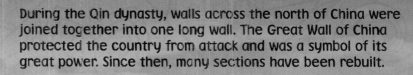

During the Qin dynasty, walls across the north of China were joined together into one long wall. The Great Wall of China protected the country from attack and was a symbol of its great power. Since then, many sections have been rebuilt.

Facts and figures

The Shang used cowry shells as currency.

One Shang bronze pot, the 'Houmuwu', weighs 875 kilograms. That's around the same weight as two horses!

Lady Fu Hao was buried with sixteen servants and six dogs.

Historians think that the Shang may have sacrificed at least 13,000 people during the final 250 years of their rule.

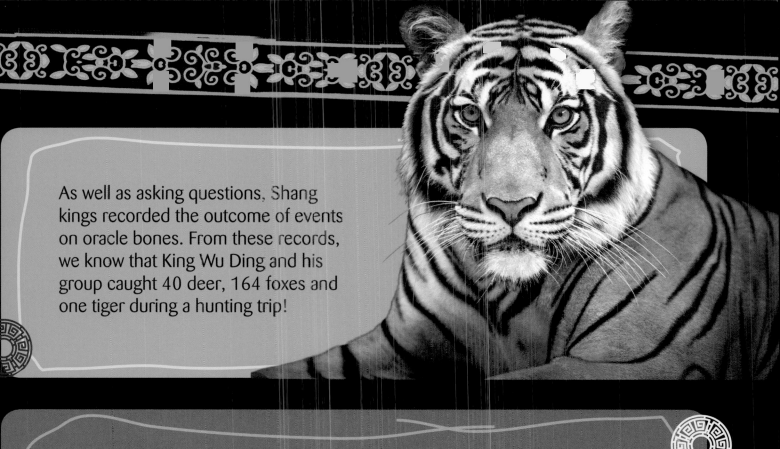

As well as asking questions, Shang kings recorded the outcome of events on oracle bones. From these records, we know that King Wu Ding and his group caught 40 deer, 164 foxes and one tiger during a hunting trip!

Timeline

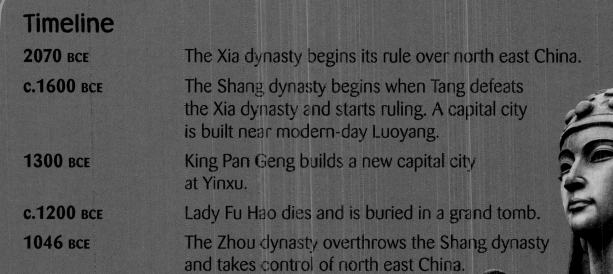

2070 BCE	The Xia dynasty begins its rule over north east China.
c.1600 BCE	The Shang dynasty begins when Tang defeats the Xia dynasty and starts ruling. A capital city is built near modern-day Luoyang.
1300 BCE	King Pan Geng builds a new capital city at Yinxu.
c.1200 BCE	Lady Fu Hao dies and is buried in a grand tomb.
1046 BCE	The Zhou dynasty overthrows the Shang dynasty and takes control of north east China.
221 BCE	The Qin dynasty takes control.
CE 19th century and 20th centuries	'Dragon bones' are found to be ancient Shang oracle bones. Historians uncover new information about the Shang dynasty.

29

Glossary

afterlife The life that begins after death

alliance A different group of people who have agreed to work with you for a common cause

ancestors People from your family who lived a long time ago

archaeologists People who learn about the past by digging up old objects

artefact An object from the past that reveals information about the people who made it

BCE The letters 'BCE' stand for 'before common era'. They refer to dates before CE 1.

casting The process of using moulds to shape metal objects

CE The letters 'CE' stand for 'common era'. They refer to dates from CE 1.

climate The weather conditions in an area

consult To get information from someone about a particular subject

currency The money used in a country or area

diviner Someone who predicts the future

dynasty A series of rulers from the same family

fertile Describes land in which you can grow good-quality crops

foundation The underground structure that supports a building

grave goods Objects that are placed in a person's tomb for use in the afterlife

jade A precious green stone

molten Melted

natural disaster An event that isn't caused by humans that creates a lot of damage, such as an earthquake

nomadic Describes someone who moves around instead of living in one place

oracle bone A bone with questions written on it which the Shang used to tell the future

ore Rock or soil from which metal can be obtained

peasant A poor person from the past

rammed-earth Layers of earth which are pressed together to make walls

refine To make a material pure by removing other substances from it

ritual A religious ceremony where certain actions are carried out

sacrifice The act of killing an animal or a person because you believe it will make a god happy

taotie An animal mask design seen on many Shang bronze pots

territory An area of land that is ruled by a particular leader or group of people

tomb A room, often underground, where someone is buried

vessel A container for liquids

Further reading

The Shang Dynasty of Ancient China (The History Detective Investigates),
Geoff Barker (Wayland, 2015)

The Shang and other Chinese Dynasties (Technology in the Ancient World)
Charlie Samuels (Franklin Watts, 2015)

Shang Dynasty China (Great Civilisations)
Tracey Kelly (Franklin Watts, 2016)

Websites

http://etcweb.princeton.edu/asianart/interactives/bronze/bronze.html
Design your own Shang-style bronze pot.

http://www.metmuseum.org/toah/hd/shzh/hd_shzh.htm#/slideshow1
Look at a slideshow of Shang artefacts from the Metropolitan Museum in New York.

http://www.ancientchina.co.uk/writing/challenge/cha_set.html
Play a game to identify some symbols from ancient Chinese writing.

http://www.dkfindout.com/uk/history/ancient-china/
An in-depth guide to China after the Qin dynasty.

Index